Can You Put on Your T-shirt?

Seed Learning

Can you put on your T-shirt?

Yes, I can.

I can put on
my T-shirt.

Can you put on your pants?

Yes, I can.

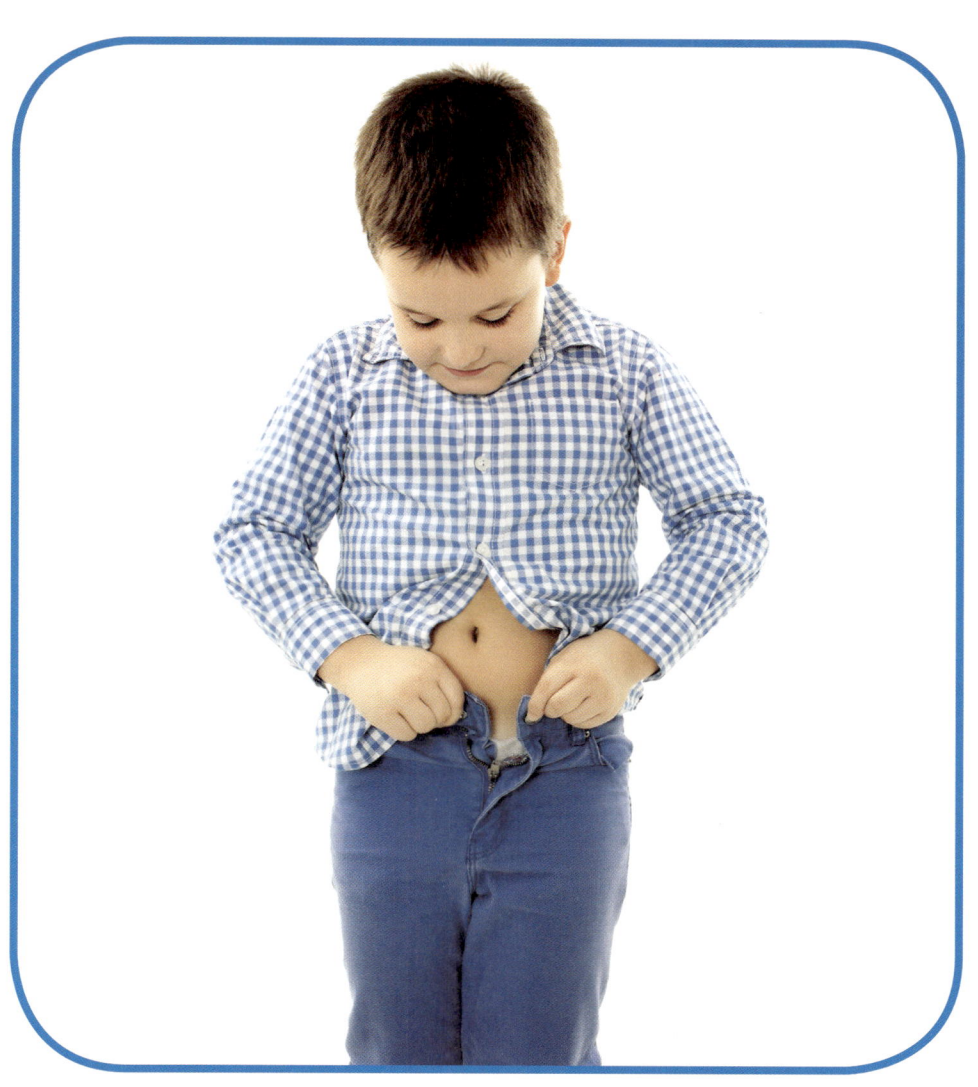

I can put on
my pants.

Can you put on your socks?

Yes, I can.

I can put on
my socks.

Can you put on your shoes?

Yes, I can.

I can put on
my shoes.

Can you put on your hat?

Yes, I can.

I can put on
my hat.

Can you put on your gloves?

Yes, I can.

I can put on
my gloves.

Can you put on your jacket?

Yes, I can.

I can put on
my jacket.

Let's learn about Cinco de Mayo.

May

Sunday	Monday	Tuesday	Wednesday	Thursday	Friday	Saturday
					1	2
3	4	(5)	6	7	8	9
10	11	12	13	14	15	16
17	18	19	20	21	22	23
24	25	26	27	28	29	30
31						

Trace the word May
and circle the date.